SECRETS TO CREATING WEALTH

Learn How To Create Outrageous Wealth With Only 2 Pennies To Rub Together!

by Stephen Pierce

SECRETS TO CREATING WEALTH

By Stephen Pierce

1-933596-01-5   Secrets to Creating Wealth by Stephen A. Pierce (Hardcover)

1-933596-02-3   Secrets to Creating Wealth by Stephen A. Pierce (Audio)

1-933596-41-4   Secrets to Creating Wealth by Stephen A. Pierce (Paperback)

Published by:

MORGAN · JAMES
PUBLISHING FOR THE REST OF US...

Morgan James Publishing, LLC

1225 Franklin Ave Ste 325

Garden City, NY 11530-1693

Toll Free 800-485-4943

www.MorganJamesPublishing.com

Cover and Inside Design by:
Heather Kirk
www.GraphicsByHeather.com
Heather@GraphicsByHeather.com

Habitat
for Humanity®
Peninsula
Building Partner

Acknowledgements

I'd like to give praise to my Lord and Saviour Jesus Christ who is my rock. With him all things are possible. I'd like to thank my lovely wife Alicia (my biggest fan) who keeps me driven daily with passion and purpose. To my sister-in-law Lorette and my incredible team, Ilona, Dad Lyttle, Teddy, Laura, and Lindsey, thank you. To my in-laws, thanks for all your support. To my parents Alice and Lander Pierce, my sisters April and Gloria, and brother Thomas. I love and appreciate you all. Thank you to my mentor Mike Murdock, your wisdom teaching has inspired me more than you'll ever know. To Joel Osteen, Dave Martin, Anthony Robbins, Paul Scheele and John Assaraf, thank you for your inspiration and enlightenment. To my friends online and offline, thanks for your support.

To you, the reader who has picked up this book, thank you for your support. May the words on these pages leap off, become real and assist you in transforming your life of dreams into a living reality.

Success is sweet, but sharing it is even sweeter, so it's within these pages that I share with you the secrets of creating wealth…

God Bless YOU and YOURS,

Stephen A. Pierce

Foreword

I am absolutely fired up. I am absolutely jazzed up. I am absolutely passionate and overflowing with enthusiasm right now.

You're saying, "Mike, why are you so excited?" I'm going to tell you about that in a second. For those who don't know who I am — my name is Mike Litman. I'm the number one best-selling author of *Conversations With Millionaires*, and over the last four years, we've been able to change the lives of more than 275,000 people.

When the great Stephen Pierce told me about this CD set and book he was putting together, I asked him, I begged him, I pleaded with him to allow me to do a small introduction before you get shaking and baking. You're asking why, over the last two years, Stephen Pierce has had an incredibly powerful and radically positive impact on my life and on my business.

Over the last few years, I've been able to hang out and interview people like Tony Robbins, well-known CEOs, and some of the top executive and successful people in the world.

I'm here to tell you something important and something that you need to listen to closely and carefully, because you need to hear this:

Stephen Pierce is one of the top entrepreneurs I've ever met in my life. His rags-to-riches story will inspire you. His story, his principles, and what he's going to outline for you — his secrets of creating wealth — are going to change your life.

This is a book that you are going to want to read over and over and over again. Stephen Pierce owns multiple businesses, both online and off-line, doing millions of dollars of sales a year. He's made hundreds of thousands of dollars in one day, and he's touched the lives of hundreds of thousands of people. He has touched my life. In this book you are about to hear book you are about to read, he is going to incredibly touch your life, as well. Sit back, grab your favorite beverage, and enjoy the genius of the great Stephen Pierce.

~ Mike Litman

Table of Contents

Welcome to the "Secrets of Creating Wealth"

These key insights into creating wealth have transformed my life from a devastating and vicious cycle of poverty to an incredibly humbling lifestyle of prosperity and success. Nothing in my past indicated that the life I live today would even be possible.

I got my family evicted from an apartment complex when I was only 12 years old. I dropped out of high school with a 10th grade education. I filed for bankruptcy not once, but twice. I was homeless for three months, sleeping on the floor of an empty office space. I took "baths" (more like washing up) in the sinks of the building's bathrooms. I tried my hand at several businesses, and they all failed miserably.

The facts of my life started to frighten me. I remember when a family member looked into my eyes and said, "Everything you touch in life turns to dust." I felt abandoned; I felt helpless and hopeless. I had no cheerleaders. No one was saying, "You can do it." Instead, people were wondering when I was going to die. In fact, at one point I was hanging out on the streets with the wrong crowd and ended up getting shot. At the time, my associates on the street said that I was basically marked for death.

But you know what? The Lord spared my life. Instead of being shot in the head, I was shot in the leg, where the bullet remains today as a reminder of what *not* to do. Actually, the bullet is still there because the hospital refused to do surgery on someone who didn't have health insurance. But for me, it's a reminder of what not to do. You don't need to be shot in the leg as a reminder. You don't need to file bankruptcy or be homeless or experience multiple, miserable business failures. It's my hope that what you discover in this book will propel you from surviving to succeeding.

What you are about to discover will reverse the lack and poverty in your life and allow you to taste the sweetness of wealth and fulfillment.

Yesterday's impossibilities are today's possibilities. I know wealth can be yours. My life is a living testament to what is possible. It doesn't matter where you are. It doesn't matter what you have in your bank account. It doesn't matter what your current assets are. I know you can have the breakthroughs you desire and have a fulfilling life.

Right now, I am happily married and our family runs several success-ful Internet companies and regular retail businesses. We create and publish our own products. Each time we release a new product, we make $100,000 or more in three days or less. One of the products we released just over a year ago has done nearly $1 million in sales all by itself. We do all this working from our home. We also have various partnerships and joint venture deals that are worth millions. One of the partnerships we just put into operation has brought in over $2 million in the last five months. Again, while working from our home.

This is not about me, but I want you to see the other side of my story — what has happened since I discovered these key strategies for creating wealth. I'm not saying this to impress you, but *to impress upon you* the possibilities that exist, regardless of your current situation. I can go on and on about the incredible success that we have been blessed with and have experienced. But let's get you up-close and personal with the power-ful discoveries that have played a massive role in turning around my life. It can happen for you. I know it can happen for you. However, you need to become fully involved with this process.

De-Stress

It's not unusual to be a little stressed out when you're starting something new. Let's take care of that before we get started. I learned a quick way to alleviate stress that's helped me over the years. It may take a little time to get the technique down, but once you do, it's an incredible stress reliever.

Start by thinking about what is causing you stress. Zero-in on it, because sometimes we can be stressed about something but not know exactly what it is. I want you to focus on the issue or issues that are causing you stress. Close your eyes and breathe in through your nose slowly and deeply. Now close both hands into tight fists in front of you or at your sides, whichever is more comfortable for you. Focus on your fists, and visualize that everything that's causing you stress is in the closed palms of your hands. Focus all those stressful things into the palms of your hands.

Now tighten your fists and squeeze harder and harder, as if you were trying to squeeze blood from them. Allow all the stress that you are experiencing to flow into your fists. Feel the stress. Tense your body. Squeeze your fists tightly and experience the stress.

Imagine that all the stress is in your hands. It is real, it is alive, and you are experiencing it in the palms of your hands, in your tightly closed fists. Now breathe out quickly through your mouth and say the word "cancel." As you open your fists, picture all of the stress disappearing out of your hands. Allow your body to become fully relaxed, and shift your mind to something that makes you happy or that could make you happy. Feel the stress released from your body.

Once you get the hang of this technique, you will see that you have the power to automatically relax your body and mind and neutralize the stress that you experience on a day-to-day basis. For many of us, stress is unavoidable. Because we're not able to avoid it, the ideal approach is to manage it so it doesn't control us.

Now that your body is relaxed, your mind is calm, and you are open and receptive to becoming wealthy beyond your wildest dreams, let's look at the Power of the Third Influence.

The Power of the Third Influence

The Third Influence is one of my personal success discoveries from years ago. Once you grasp hold of what the Third Influence is all about, you can truly accelerate positive changes in your life and get on the path to accomplishing your goals. Pay close attention to this; it is very profound.

To help you to understand what the Third Influence is all about, let's take a quick trip to the science lab. Let's say you have an objective that you want to reach. It can be a particular goal: a personal goal or a professional goal. Let's use water to represent that goal. We are starting off with two hydrogen molecules, and we know hydrogen is a gas. By themselves, the two molecules are not water. But they have the potential to become water, just like you have the potential to achieve whatever goal you would like to achieve.

We know that we need to add something else to those two hydrogen molecules in order to create water. What do we need to add? We add an oxygen molecule. Once we combine that oxygen molecule with those two hydrogen molecules, we have H_2O; we have water. That objective of creating water has been achieved.

But what happens if you take those same two hydrogen molecules and you add the wrong Third Influence? What happens if we add a totally different Third Influence to the equation? What if we add a sulfur molecule? For those who don't know, two hydrogen molecules and a sulfur molecule create what is called hydrogen sulfide or H_2S. This is a stinky gas that smells like rotten eggs. It is often referred to as sewer gas.

Hydrogen sulfide is a highly poisonous gas, whose toxicity is similar to that of cyanide. Basically, if you have the wrong Third Influence in your life, your life can be completely poisoned. You can get completely off track from what you want to accomplish.

For example, let's look at Mike Tyson. When he was very young, he had a Third Influence come into his life and it took him to the pinnacles of the heavyweight division. It actually made him the youngest heavy-weight champion ever. But what happened? Later on, a different Third Influence entered his life. It was a bad influence. He became like the stinky, poisonous gas. Things just tumbled for him.

What does that tell us? It tells us that regardless of the success we experience, we are always vulnerable to a Third Influence that can shift things. Take River Phoenix, for example. He had a Third Influence. He was a budding young star with a lot of great fans. But he dropped dead from an overdose of drugs. There was a negative Third Influence that entered his life.

How about Elvis Presley? Millions of people around the world loved him. But then this negative Third Influence came into his life, and he eventually died of a drug overdose.

Third Influences come in and completely impact your thought processes and your actions. Those Third Influences come from various sources. This is basically what we see with peer pressure in young people. Sometimes they don't know how to make decisions for themselves, so they are easily persuaded and influenced by their peers. That's how they end up doing drugs and having sex at a young age. We see an increase in teenage pregnancy. We see various negative things that happen.

Let's take somebody who is an alcoholic. A Third Influence comes into his life. He ends up getting drunk, driving drunk, and killing himself or killing other people, or both. Or take the person who has the Third Influence of drugs come into her life. She is strung-out on drugs, she loses everything, and maybe she even loses her life. What do you think happens when kids and teenagers become obsessed with the newest trendy things — shoes, clothing, or gadgets of some kind? It's the Third Influence.

Many influences come into our lives. We are influenced by movies and music. These are great and powerful persuaders that we allow to come into our lives. This isn't an issue of what kind of music you should listen to or what kind of programs you should watch. The point is this: Your Third Influences have a stronghold on what direction or path in life you take, how you think, and how your life unfolds.

What I challenge you to do is take a simple test to see how the Third Influence plays a part in your life. The results of this test are profound. The test will allow you to truly measure the effect of the Third Influence on your life.

For one week, go to sleep and leave the television on at a volume that you would normally listen if you were sitting in your room watching television. Take note how you feel throughout the following day: how you feel when you wake up, what your mood is like, what your thought processes are like, and what your level of productivity is. This is truly a profound experiment. It would be interesting to see what kind of results occur with long-term scientific research, but, for now, this is something you can observe over the short term. I'm sure that if the results were documented over a longer period of time, it would be even more profound.

After you've done the test with the television, do it with the radio for one week. Choose a radio station that plays the kind of music that you like. It can be Christian music, hip-hop music, R&B music, country music, or jazz music — any kind of music. Listen to the music while you sleep. Again, you want to chart the various responses you have: how you feel in the morning, how you feel throughout the day, what your level of productivity is, and how you act and react in various situations. Note any changes in mood and any level of irritability as well.

After that week's test, do a week with a cassette or CD of something that you want to listen to or something that you want to learn. It can be about marketing, sales, self-improvement, or anything. Play the CD in a CD player that has continuous play, or play the cassette in a cassette player that has auto reverse. This way, the CD or cassette will continue to play all night long, until you wake up and turn it off. Do this every single night for seven straight nights. Again, take note of how you feel in the morning, what your thought processes are throughout the day, what your level of productivity is, and all those things. You are going to find truly profound things start to happen in your life.

I found that when I have the television or radio on all night, I'm nowhere near as sharp, focused, and efficient throughout the day as when I've had some kind of personal development cassette or CD playing all night long. In fact, sometimes these crazy things start to jump into my head — lines from a Seinfeld episode or songs that pop into my head out of the blue. I can be reading a book and a thought just pops into my head. I know that something must have been playing overnight that put the line or song into my head on the subconscious level and now it's popping up. I found that my efficiency and productivity — although they are still good — are nowhere near as good as when I have some kind of positive personal development cassette or CD playing overnight.

This is something you need to try on your own. I have tried sleeping while listening to nothing, the television, music, and personal develop-ment CDs. Now, I actually like to go to sleep with headphones on, listen-ing to all different types of things. I love to listen to praise and worship music. I also like to listen to a lot of teaching cassettes and CDs.

But that's me. I want you to take the challenge for yourself and see how it affects your own life. You are going to find that by maximizing the use of your sleep time, you can actually help to accelerate your learning. You can help to accelerate your productivity and keep your mind sharper throughout the day when you are awake.

It is amazing how you feel the next day. Your thinking becomes clearer in various situations, you become much more creative, you are able to handle problems much better, and your irritability diminishes. This is how a Third Influence affects your life. It's okay if you play nothing; it's just a night of sleep. You're going to wake up and feel however it is you're going to feel.

When it comes down to the Third Influence, a chain reaction takes place. You can see this in young people, in business, and in the pursuit of wealth of all kinds. You can also see how people take advantage of others through scams and other con games.

Something occurs to get your attention. It could be someone trying to get you into some kind of multi-level marketing (MLM) or business opportunity, or someone trying to sell you on something personal or professional — whatever the case may be.

Then something happens. You start to accept what has gotten your attention as probable or possible. Then you start to be persuaded by the idea. As you move through that persuasion process, you start to enter the adoption process. You adopt that idea, person, or belief and accept it as your own. From that adoption process, you have an outcome.

This is nothing against certain business opportunities. This is not about being anti-music or anti-television. This is about understanding that in your life there is this thing called the Third Influence that has an extremely powerful impact on your life.

You need to understand that you have the power and ability to choose and control the Third Influence that shapes your actions, thought processes, and ultimately, the destination you are going to reach in your life.

Let's take the marijuana smoking and paint sniffing that young people might do. Look at the process that takes place: Something happens that gets their attention. They're not doing it, but it gets their attention. Maybe the "In" crowd or the coolest guys are doing it — and they start to associate the cool factor with it. They start to accept it because this is something that's cool. They've accepted cool, and now they are being persuaded. They're being persuaded that this is something that they should do. If they do it, they are going to be cool, too. They want to be cool, so they adopt the behavior. Guess what happens? They start to sniff the paint, smoke the marijuana, smoke the cigarettes, drink the alcohol, and engage in sex at a very, very young age. Then we ultimately have this outcome: They're hooked on drugs. They're strung out. They have broken homes, drunk driving, teenage pregnancies, and all kinds of destructive outcomes.

There is this Third Influence that takes place in our lives, and we have the ability to choose and control this Third Influence. We also have the ability to counteract the Third Influence. Maybe we can't control what kind of commercial is going to come on television or what people around us are saying, but we can control what we watch on television and the kind of people with whom we associate. We can ultimately control what we allow to be put into us by selecting the things we listen to and read.

If you want to become wealthy in real estate, what is one of the things that you should do? You should position yourself where those who have already accomplished something that you would like to accomplish can influence you. That's why I believe in coaches and mentors. They are that Third Influence that comes into your life and helps you to move closer to that place or person that you want to be.

For me, the Third Influence was one of the most profound things I had ever discovered, because when I was young I was not moving in the direction that I wanted to move. Something was wrong. I had these ideas, these dreams in my heart. I knew that I was genetically accurate and engineered to be able to accomplish those things.

But I was not moving in that direction. Something was happening that was sabotaging me, and I was not able to move in the direction that I wanted to move. I was allowing the wrong influences to come into my life. I was being influenced to do things that were not aligned with what I wanted to accomplish.

For some reason, I was influenced by ads for quick riches, overnight success, making money doing nothing, making money doing nothing fast, making money doing next to nothing, and making money working an hour a day. That was not the route that I was supposed to take. I couldn't accomplish the things I wanted to achieve by chasing down quick schemes. It wasn't going to happen. Eventually, I found out that the only person making money in those situations was the person selling the information.

I was trying to achieve certain things. I had an objective in my head. I knew that it was something I could accomplish. I knew that I was genetically accurate for it. I knew that I was engineered for it. I knew that I had the talents and skills to achieve it. But for some reason, my actions were not fully aligned to achieve what I was meant to do. My thought processes were not fully aligned. I wasn't thinking the way I needed to be thinking. That's when I started to read books and to reprogram my mind to develop the kind of mindset those who had already accomplished what I wanted to accomplish had.

Ask yourself what you want to accomplish in your life. What is that goal? What is that objective? Now ask yourself if your mentality, physiology, and actions are aligned. Are you aligned properly and congruently with what is necessary to accomplish your goals? Or are you being influenced — either by choice or not? If you don't choose what you are influenced by, you are going to be influenced by anything.

Instead of taking control of the ship and choosing where it's going, you're just a passenger on the ship going wherever the wind blows. You will drift around in life and whatever happens as a result of these random influences is what's going to happen in your life. Are you being influenced by the wrong information? Those who transfer information can also transfer misinformation. You have to watch what you allow to influence you.

Unfortunately, there are a lot of people in this world who will scam you and give you bad information, some deliberately, some accidentally. But the end result is the same, isn't it? Somebody can be very sincere in giving you directions on how to get somewhere, and they can be wrong. Somebody can be trying to be devious and give you bad directions deliberately to throw you off your path. Both sets of directions are bad, and you don't get to where you want to go. You waste time.

The point is that you need to make sure when you choose your Third Influence that you choose somebody who has a proven track record of success. Choose someone who you know you can follow and model yourself after. That's why I encourage you to go beyond the *Secrets of Creating Wealth*. Ask yourself: What is it that I truly want to accomplish? What is it that I want my life to be like? Who has accomplished that already? Who can I bring into my life to influence me? You may not be able to get into their personal inner circle — like going to their house or something like that — but you can read their books. You can watch their videos, go to seminars, and listen to audio programs. That's a very strong starting point. I encourage you to do it immediately and regularly.

Take the time to think about what you really want your life to look and be like. When it comes down to it, this is what we have. This is what the Third Influence looks like. There are two Hs. Just like we had those two hydrogen molecules in our example earlier, we have our other two Hs when it comes to you and me as people. We have two hows: *How* you are now and *How* you want to be. The Third Influence is going to have a tremendous, dramatic impact on what you actually become. Is it exactly how you want to be or completely different?

You are going to become either the water or the stinky gas that smells like rotten eggs. You have the ability and power to choose what your Third Influence is going to be. Take control of that. Every single day block out a half hour or an hour and allow yourself to be deliberately influenced by a certain pool of information that will help you move closer to what you want to become.

First you need to figure out what you want. Is it real estate? Is it investing? Is it franchising? Is it running a business on the Internet? Is it having a happier household? A stronger marriage? Is it having a healthier body? You need to find out exactly what it is. Be absolutely clear about what you want to be and how you want to be. Don't think about whether something is going to be impossible to accomplish. This is neither the time nor place to think about what is possible or impossible. Remember one thing: Yesterdays impossibilities are today's possibilities.

I want you to focus on only one thing right now: What is that one thing that you want to be? How do you want your life to be? I know that we want to improve ourselves spiritually, physically, mentally, socially, emotionally, intellectually, and sexually. We are complex human beings, and we can be fulfilled in one area of our life and for some reason we are still unhappy because we feel unfulfilled in another area of our life. For right now, focus on just one thing. Later you can focus on each area of your life one at a time and experience a total level of fulfillment in all of those different areas where you would like to see improvement.

We don't want to complicate the process right now, and we definitely don't want to be overwhelmed by the various changes we want to make in our life. Change is a process, and the process should be fun. We should enjoy the various changes that we see along the way.

The Power of the Third Influence

Ask yourself how you want to be in "X" area of your life. Let's say it is how you want to be financially. Let's say you want to make $100,000 a year. That's relatively easy nowadays. Let's say that you are in sales, and you want to make $100,000 a year. Let's say that currently you are making $50,000 a year. Basically, what you want to do is double your income. Think about which salespeople you know who make $100,000 a year in your organization or in your industry or in some other kind of industry. Then you do something that we call "borrowed genius," which entails looking in other places, other organizations or other industries to borrow processes to adopt. You amplify them, and you modify them; you put your own spin on them. See how you can adjust and adapt the processes to your environment and your business to improve your results.

When you find out who in your organization is already making $100,000 a year, find out what they're doing. Find out their processes. Talk with them. Find some of the top sales trainers that come into your organization to help to train these people and contact them directly; get their materials. Get some one-on-one coaching from them if you can. Do whatever it takes to fully align yourself with reaching that goal of doubling your income.

Look at timeframes and set a deadline for reaching your goal. You don't want to double your income in 10 years. That's way too long. Maybe you want to double your income in one year. You need to figure out what you want and get down to the micro detail. Look at the details regarding how many more prospects you need to call, how many more sales presentations you need to make, and how you can refine your openings, closings, and dealing with objections. Look at the sales people who know how best to deal with objections in your industry. Model yourself after that.

Who are the people that are the most formidable and awesome closers in your industry or in any industry? Align yourself with those people and adopt their skills. What is happening is this: You are allowing that Third

Influence in your life to put you right on track and get you aligned and congruent in your actions and thought processes in what you want to accomplish. In this example, what you want to accomplish is doubling your income as a salesperson from $50,000 to $100,000.

You need to understand that in your life there is a Third Influence. Whether or not you want to accept it is up to you. But the Third Influence is not going to go away. Ask yourself what you are allowing to influence you, either by choice or by not choosing to do anything. The Third Influence is there.

Take the time to deliberately decide what you are going to allow yourself to be influenced by. What you decide you will be influenced by depends upon what your objectives are. Take the time to find out what your objectives are in the various areas of your life. You want to stretch yourself, but don't stretch yourself too far. You don't want to set goals that are so lofty and so far out there that you get discouraged in the process of achieving them.

For example, a person may want to lose 100 pounds, and loses only 25 or 50 pounds. He hits a plateau and can't seem to lose the other 50 pounds. He becomes discouraged because he didn't lose 100 pounds. But that's not right, because he didn't even celebrate the fact that he *did lose* the 25 or 50 pounds.

We sabotage ourselves because we don't celebrate the small successes on the road to achieving the big objective. When you lose 100 pounds, you do it one pound at a time. If you break it down into smaller goals, you have to lose one ounce at a time. You need to celebrate each pound that you lose. If you want to lose 100 pounds, and you lost one pound, guess what? You are now only 99 pounds away from reaching that objective. You have to look at it that way, because each one of those small successes can give you momentum and confidence to stay the course and continue to pursue what you want to accomplish.

If you reach some kind of plateau — whether it is in your income, business, health, or weight-loss — you need to adjust and figure out what you need to do to break through that plateau. People who are in weightlifting sometimes reach a plateau where they can't bench press or squat more weight. They make certain adjustments in their exercise routine so that they can break through those particular plateaus. Don't get discouraged if you reach a plateau. Find out who has gotten beyond the plateau where you are stuck and allow yourself to be influenced by that person.

Make sure that whatever you choose to be, that deliberate Third Influence in your life is a pure source. Make sure it is a source that has accomplished the things that you want to accomplish. People are great sources of a Third Influence, but if you want to achieve $100,000 a year as a salesperson, you have to learn from a salesperson who is making $250,000 a year. You can network with them, but you need to make sure that you are moving vertically, not horizontally. When you are moving vertically, you don't want to move down. This is not about being better than somebody else. It's not that somebody who is making less than you are is not good enough to associate with. I'm talking about aligning yourself with those who have been there, done that, and have maybe even moved beyond what it is you want to achieve. Allow yourself to be influenced by their habits, their mindset, their skill set, their wisdom, their knowledge, and their understanding.

From this day forward, you are going to deliberately decide every single day what is going to influence you. You are going to take the necessary actions. At a minimum, you are going to block out 30 minutes of your day to make sure that you're influenced by some kind of cassette, video, or book that can move you closer to how you want to be. Remember, how you are now does not mean you have to stay that way.

However you feel about yourself right now — good, bad, or indifferent — there is a much bigger world out there. You are genetically accurate for success. You are engineered for success. You have got the goods, and you can accomplish it. Don't allow yourself to be sabotaged by ignoring the power of the Third Influence. From this point on you are deliberately deciding what you are going to be influenced by, and you are going to use it for your betterment and empowerment and to help you accelerate yourself towards being what you want to be.

Success Habits

Let's talk about your habits. Mike Murdock, one of my mentors, says that habit is more powerful than desire. What you do habitually will determine what you become permanently. Many would-be millionaires and success creators and those who have the birthright to experience wealth join MLM program after MLM program. They hop from one program to the next and from one business opportunity to the next. Some create a home-based business, a brick-and-mortar business, or an Internet business — all out of the desire to create wealth and to experience financial success.

You know what? That is your birthright. You have the right to experience financial success. However, that desire for financial success continues to be swallowed up by the habits of doing nothing, laziness, and making excuses for why right now is not the best time to do what needs to be done. These destructive habits eat away at the desire for success: the habits of procrastination, organization without productive action, looking for shortcuts, looking for the easy way, looking for the get-rich-quick method. I'm sure you know people with these habits. Habits can quickly fan the flames of your burning desires, while choking the life out of your dreams of wealth, success, and prosperity.

Some people actually do things; they market their products, join MLM programs, or start a home-based business, but they don't do it consistently. The habit of being inconsistent paralyzes their marketing efforts. It paralyzes their sales efforts. Your dreams of wealth and financial success are at risk of being destroyed if you don't quickly cultivate the success habits that will support and invigorate them. You will carry all of your dreams to your grave, unfulfilled, if you continue to bow to those destructive habits that serve only one purpose — to strangle your dreams.

It doesn't matter what your dream is — it can be to be an athlete, a musician, or a corporate mover and shaker. Your dream may be to become a successful dad or mom, or to have a successful family. It doesn't matter what the dream is; it is not that you don't want it enough. It is not that you are not sincere enough about your dream. It is not even that you are incapable of accomplishing those desires and fulfilling those dreams. It is that your desires are being sabotaged by your self-defeating, dream-imploding habits. You must identify those habits quickly and make changes. You cannot ignore them or think that everything is going to be okay.

What you cannot correct and what you are unwilling to confront is going to dominate your life. It will control you. You can look at any mentor. Think of somebody who inspires you, somebody who you want to emulate, whose life inspires you to want to be something. Think of that person. They inspire you to want to be better. They inspire you to want more. They inspire you to want the best for yourself and for your family. They really motivate you. One of your heartfelt desires can be to emulate them, to experience the level of success, or even just a portion of the success, that they have experienced. Maybe you want to be like them. But there is no way to be like them if you don't adopt the success habits that they have.

The person who inspires you may be able to sit at the beach right now and work only a couple hours a day or a few seasons or throughout a season if he or she is an athlete. However, I can assure you that it has not always been that way for that person. It doesn't matter who you name. You can name your marketing guru, your athletic icon, or your business icon. I can assure you that the road to where they are now is paved with the habit of daily sweat, focused energy, concentrated labor, and very specific tasks designed to build their dream and to fulfill their desires.

Think of Michael Jordan. The love that people have for him has no bounds. It crosses all racial lines and international borders. However, the lonely path that he took to that success — the rejection, the hard work by himself at the gym and on the court while going years without a championship ring — is just as much a part of the dream that Mike has right now as when he was active in the NBA. All of that is just as much a part of him today as all those awards, the money, the honor, the glamour, and the celebrity that he experiences. Without that, he would not be where he is today.

It is all part of the package. Sacrifices and sweat — all the things that may seem to be inconvenient or that move you outside of your comfort zone — are par for the course. So is changing bad habits to good habits and changing habits of sabotage to constructive habits. Everybody has to do that. The worst thing you can do is think that you don't have to change your habits to accommodate the dream that you want to pursue.

You have to focus on making sure that everything is congruent in your life to support the dreams and desires that you have, to see those things be transformed from the dream state into the reality state. Until you can understand and appreciate what your mentors have gone through to get where they are, it is almost impossible to fully understand their success and what it means. Look at somebody like Oprah or Donald Trump or anybody who has a great life and whom you want to be like.

There is nothing wrong with having mentors or wanting to be like somebody. But you must understand the path that they took and what they had to go through to get where they are. Where somebody is right now — whatever part of his or her life that you are in contact with, from a distance or from the inside — was reached through a process. They had a starting point and they stayed the course. The big picture of success contains much more than just a destination or arriving at a certain point. For most people, the destination is something that they never had before. They cherish the moments. They bask in the fact that they have been able to achieve what they have been able to achieve. You are no different. I know that there are certain dreams in your heart that are ready to be brought forth, that you want to experience, that you have never experienced before.

I love the saying: If you want something that you've never had before, you have to do things that you've never done before. If you keep doing what you're doing, you're going to keep getting the same thing you've got. Mike Murdock says: "The secret of your wealth is hidden in your daily routine. What you do habitually will impact what you become permanently." Let me ask you: Do you repeatedly put off starting specific tasks that can have a huge impact on your life, success, and wealth?

Do you sporadically do certain things that if you did them consistently and regularly could have a huge impact on your life, success, and wealth? Do you constantly procrastinate? Do you hop from one business opportunity to the next, from one MLM program to the next, or from one idea to the next? Do you always seek get-rich-quick schemes? Do you always have to play the number, hoping that one day you will be watching television and your number is going to be called? The bottom line is that what your daily routine consists of is going to impact what you become permanently. What does your daily routine consist of? What are you doing on a daily basis?

Think about everything you've done today and then think about what your truest dreams are. Of the things you've done today, how many went towards the advancement of your dream? How many of those things have any kind of direct impact on your dreams being transformed into reality? If you tell me what you do habitually, I can tell you with a great deal of certainty what you are most likely to become permanently.

What you do and what you don't do daily has a huge impact on what you become permanently. You need to start to align your days and the activities in your days with what your real objectives are. Stop running around aimlessly thinking that things are just going to happen. That's not how it works. Stop putting off until tomorrow something that you can do today. Not something that you *can do* today, but something that you *must do* today if you want to realize your dreams.

You must do certain things today if you ever expect to advance forward and closer to your objective. You can't continue to put it off. The world is not going to wait for you. You are a not going to get any younger. Each second, each hour, each day that goes by is time that you are losing that you will never be able to retrieve. Don't do that to yourself.

There is a saying: There is no tomorrow, because by the time it gets here it is called today. Today is all you have — nothing else. The actions that you take and don't take right now decide where your life is going to be or where it is not going to be. There's a quote that had a major impact on my thinking process: "Yesterday is a canceled check, tomorrow is a promissory note, but today is cash on hand." Think about that for a minute. "Yesterday is a canceled check, tomorrow is a promissory note, but today is cash on hand."

Your most precious resource is your time. That is it. What you do or don't do with it has a huge impact on your life. If there was ever a sin against our dreams and desires, it is the squandering of those 24 golden boxcars that are the 24 hours in a day.

24 Hours
Respect Your Dreams

What are you putting into your 24 golden boxcars? Are you putting in dirt, rubble, or hay? What are you doing with the 24 hours that you are allotted every single day? What mental crutch are you using as an excuse for your procrastination and, even worse, your misappropriation of those 24 hours?

In corporate America, the misappropriation of funds is illegal. But the misappropriation of those 24 hours in your life is worse; it's almost unforgivable. Your life will not forgive you. When you squander those hours, you can never get them back.

The negative impact of the misuse or the unproductive use of those hours ripples throughout your family and your life. It ripples through all the people who have contact with you and your family.

Have you ever thought about the impact what you do has on those around you? What would it mean to you if your dreams were transformed into reality? What would it mean to you and your family if you actually experienced the reality of those dreams? How important is it that you experience those dreams and that they be transformed into reality? What would it mean to you to have those breakthroughs and start to experience the changes? What would that mean to you?

It is possible. Think about what you are filling those 24 hours with each day. The way you use each hour of your day shows what you value and what is most important to you.

What you respect — not what you need, want, desire, or love — you will attract. What you don't respect, you will lose. If you are married or if you are dating, you can need, desire, and love your mate, but if you disrespect your mate, you are likely to lose your mate. If you are disrespected, what do you do? Do you stay or do you leave?

If you had a business partner who never showed up for meetings or was constantly late, and he was disrespectful to you, your time, and your business, what would you do? Depending on the legal structure of the relationship, you may not be able to quickly terminate it, or maybe you would. But it would certainly strain the relationship, wouldn't it?

The same goes for your dreams and your desires. It doesn't matter how good they make you feel when you close your eyes and envision them. It doesn't matter how sure you are that you have the ability to achieve them. I am going to tell you right now: You have the ability to achieve your dreams. At least, in your present state you have a certain ability to achieve a part of them that will get you to the point where you can continue to develop, grow, and enhance your abilities to achieve some of your higher goals. This isn't a question of your ability to achieve your goals.

It doesn't matter how hot an opportunity or how big a ground-floor opportunity it may be, if you fail to respect your dreams and your desires by habitually doing the daily tasks that grind up against them, that don't support them, then you have literally ripped the heart out of those dreams and desires. I can assure you that their pulse is weak and they are soon going to be flat lined, dead, and gone.

For your desires to manifest themselves into reality, you need to breathe life into them and get them moving. You need to feed them and you need to nurture them. You do this by developing a solid and unshakable daily habit of performing those tasks you need to perform in order to see that the seeds of your dreams are birthed and that they grow. You can't say that you respect your dreams and your desires and not allocate the required hours in your day to go about those important routine tasks, regardless of how routine they may be. They may be critical to the materialization of your dreams. If you are not doing those tasks, how can you say that you respect your dreams? How can you say that you respect your desires?

You are engaging in wishful thinking if all you are doing is thinking that it would be great to have this or that or to be like this or that person, but you are not adopting the habits that got that person to where they are. If you are continuing to do what you are doing and you are in a present state of poverty, or you are feeling as if you are an underachiever, and not accomplishing or experiencing your dreams, you need to wake up and realize that you are not going to get any closer to living your dream by continuing to do what you're doing. You need to stop allowing yourself to suffer from negative habits.

What must you do today to move your business or your life forward in the direction that can ignite financial success and transform your dreams and desires into reality? You need to create the habits of success that will support your dreams, your visions, and your desires.

Your Habits Decide Your Future

Do you want to know one of the differences between someone who is experiencing a great deal of success in their life and someone who isn't? There are many differences, but one clear difference is that those who are successful make decisions that create the *future* they desire, while unsuccessful people make decisions that create the *present* they desire.

Procrastination gives an unsuccessful person some kind of immediate sense of pleasure that creates the present they desire. But it is only delaying the pain. A successful person takes very specific and directed action to create the future that he or she desires, regardless of how painful it is to do right now. In the future they are going to experience the life that they have designed for themselves. It is often stated that habits are the easiest things to create but the hardest things to break. What you do not master will master you. If you do not control your habits, your habits will end up controlling you. But there is hope.

You can break any bad habit. You can break and disrupt any damaging pattern that has you spinning your wheels and bumping your head against the wall. This message is meant to be more than motivating; it is meant to detonate an explosive amount of action within you to start evaluating your life and creating new habits. You don't have to make huge changes; you can start with something small. Start with something that is manageable so that when you make that change and you start adopting the new habit, you will feel a sense of success and progress. Don't try to make huge, massive changes in your life. You can change one small thing in your life and it can have a huge, dramatic impact.

For example, if a person who is overweight habitually eats pizza at midnight before going to sleep, what you think is going to happen to his waistline? Let's say that the person didn't adopt the habit of regular exercise, but first started with changing the timing of when he ate. He stopped eating really heavy, fatty foods before he went to bed. That is a really small change that can have a big impact on his weight. He will have to do something much more than that to reach his ultimate goal, but it is a start. Maybe he starts snacking on fruit or vegetables instead of cookies or chips.

That person can go out and buy a bunch of exercise equipment, go on a vegetarian organic diet, get a Stairmaster and a membership at a health club, but that's not what it's about. You can make incremental, gradual changes that will have an exponential, explosive impact on your life, health, finances, and family.

You need to decide which things need to be changed. Which habits are not supporting you? Which habits are damaging? Which habits are para-lyzing your progress? Which habits are choking the life out of your dreams? You need to take the time to identify those habits. Picture when you want to accomplish your goal. Look at what you're doing on a daily, weekly, and monthly basis, and adjust your habits using a process of elimination. Ask yourself what is not supporting your path to your destination.

Some habits are difficult to break. Those habits are damaging because you get caught in a powerful cycle and your body resists breaking the habits. But that is not an excuse for not breaking the habits. You can change the habits.

One of the best ways to eliminate bad habits is to create new good habits that override and replace the bad ones. Instead of trying to totally eliminate a bad habit, see if there's a way you can replace it.

Let's take food, for example. If you eat a lot of sugary foods and have a sweet tooth, and you need to quit eating like that for your health or to lose weight, there are a lot of good snacks and treats you can eat in place of the really bad sugary foods. You can still take care of your sweets cravings. It's the same with fatty foods. You can find some really good organic, low-carb, prepackaged meals that taste good and can replace a lot of bad fats you are putting into your body.

Start making changes in those bad or destructive habits because, like it or not, your habits are going to determine your future. What daily routine must you start right now? Add something more and replace something that's ineffective or damaging. You don't need to make huge mega-shifts in your life. Think about what you have been putting off every day that has been crippling your life, business, or sales process, if you're a salesperson. What have you been putting off that you need to start doing? You can start doing it a little bit at a time. But whatever it is, you need to *start* doing it. You need to start identifying all the habits that are damaging you and that are silently killing your dream.

Intolerance of your present condition can ignite change, just as tolerance of your current condition can prevent change. If you ignore your bad habits and don't take an inventory of the things you need to change, you are silently accepting and tolerating your current condition. That is going to prevent you from changing. You have no one to blame but yourself. You can't say that life dealt you a bad blow, gave you a bad hand, or didn't give you a fair opportunity. It is simply not true that every single successful person who is walking, has walked, or will walk the face of this earth and who is living the life of their dreams was dealt a hand that was in their favor. If you believe that, you are deceiving yourself. That is not how it goes.

A bodybuilder doesn't just walk on stage as Mr. Olympia. Some body-builders may have good genes, but all of them have to put in a lot of work and a lot of discipline with their diet and training schedule to get to that point. It is not automatic just because they want it. It is not automatic just because they have good genes. They still have to put in the required work.

This is all on you right now. What are you going to do? When I say that it is all on you, it doesn't mean that you are all by yourself; but it is all on you because nobody can make your decisions for you. Nobody can make you make changes. Nobody can make you decide that enough is enough. Nobody can make you say, "I am fed up with where my life is. I am fed up with allowing myself to defeat myself. I am fed up with silently letting these habits control me and direct my destiny."

Get fed up, but also make a change. Again, you don't have to start with huge changes. Decide on a bunch of small changes, line them up and start picking them off one by one. Identify those bad habits; replace them with some good habits.

It is amazing when you start to make those small changes. It does something for your self-esteem and your mental health. It feeds off of itself and you start to build up momentum and you accelerate in the direction you actually want to go.

But before you can experience any acceleration or any momentum moving you in the direction you want to move, you have to start moving. You have to start doing something. You can't drive a car until you get in, stick the key in the ignition and turn it, put the car in drive, and put your foot on the gas. You need to start making these little changes to your habits. If you remember only one thing, remember this: You decide your habits. Your habits decide your future.

Change Takes Time and Patience

You cannot be what you are not, but you can become what you are not. It is like the caterpillar that has its moment in time and undergoes that incredible transformation, that metamorphosis, and becomes the beautiful butterfly. It takes on a whole new look, it has beautiful colors and wings, and it can travel to places that it wasn't able to get to by crawling. The caterpillar couldn't *be* the butterfly, but it could *become* the butterfly.

Many people go through life experiencing huge levels of frustration because they are trying to be something that they are not instead of focusing on the process of *becoming* what they are not. They use credit to cannibalize their future cash because they are trying to live a certain lifestyle that they don't have the cash to live today. Instead of focusing their energies and their current resources on becoming something that they are not, they paralyze an entire process because they want to be it today.

Imagine, for example, that a caterpillar had the ability to experience emotions and frustrations like we do. How frustrated would that caterpillar be if it saw that all of its friends had wings and were flying from branch to branch and hovering around? He knows those are his friends flying around, so he tries to fly around in his present state. He would be incredibly frustrated. In fact, he would probably reach a point where he was suicidal, because he could not fly around like his friends. But it is not his time yet. He is not at that state. He has not gone through that transformation. He has the potential, but he has to wait until the necessary events run their course so he can experience the transformation and become the beautiful butterfly. Instead of being frustrated, he needs to be patient and let what needs to happen run its course. Then he will become the beautiful butterfly.

What are you doing in your life that makes you extremely frustrated because you are not experiencing the things that you want to experience? Ask yourself if it is your time yet. I am not saying sit back and wait, check the clock, check your door because Ed McMahon is going to be showing up, or check your numbers because one day you're going to hit the Powerball. That's not what I'm talking about.

What I am talking about is allowing yourself to build and go through the process of becoming what you are not, instead of wanting or expecting things to occur in an instant. You can't expect incredible outcomes to occur in your life in a moment.

You have to accept that things take time. They have to run their course. Instead of being frustrated by it, identify what process in your life you need to go through so that, like the caterpillar, you can experience that transformation or that metamorphosis. You need to be patient.

I want you to repeat this: I am not far from becoming what I am not. Say it again. I am not far from becoming what I am not. Focus on the word "far." F-A-R is an acronym, and it stands for: fantasizing, actualizing, and realizing. In *Think and Grow Rich*, Napoleon Hill says, "Whatever the mind of man can conceive and believe, it can achieve."

Many of us are very good at the conceiving part. We can dream up things all day long. Some of us are okay with the believing part; however, most of us drop the ball when it comes to the achieving part. What Napoleon Hill did not say is: "Whatever the mind of man can conceive and believe, is instantly and automatically his." He said, "The mind can achieve it." The operative word there is "achieve."

One of the definitions for the word achieve is: "to attain with effort or despite difficulty." Think about that for a minute. In that quote, Napoleon Hill was actually saying, "Whatever the mind of man can conceive and believe, it can attain with effort, despite difficulty." If you put forth the necessary and consistent effort, you can achieve it. You can attain it, despite whatever difficulties you face. You are going to face difficulties along the way. Nothing in this world goes straight up or straight down.

Think about the gold market of the 1990s. It was an incredible run-up, but you don't see a straight line. You see a whole bunch of fluctuations, but it is still going up. That is pretty much what life is like. You can reach your objectives, but what is par for the course? It is the ups and downs along the way.

Despite the difficulties that are going to come your way — and they are going to come — remember that it is fire that purifies gold. The fire is going to come into your life to purify you throughout the process. If it were easy to accomplish any kind of goal in life, everybody would be successful. What really separates the weak from the strong are the flames that come into their lives or the strong winds that are blown up against them. Strong winds make for the strongest trees and the strongest timber. Extreme pressure on carbon creates diamonds.

The fire, pressures, and the strong winds are not there to discourage or destroy you or to break you down; they are there to purify you and to build you up; to extract that diamond from within you.

Life doesn't have anything against you, but it's not going to give you a free ticket. There are few people who are born into wealth. The majority of people have to earn it; they have to work for it. They have to design the kind of life they want to live. They have to pursue it. That is what

Change Takes Time and Patience

you have to do. Nobody is going to roll out the red carpet and say, "Come on and get it, baby."

It is within your reach, within your grasp, but you have to go out there and get it. Life is going to present a fair amount of challenges for you to prove your desire for your dream and to build you up in the process. One of the greatest things about accomplishing something great is the process, not the attainment of it. It is not the arrival at a particular destination; it is the journey along the way. That is where you grow and gain wisdom. That is where you grow in understanding and knowledge.

Your greatest moments and discoveries don't occur when you're winning. They come in your moments of trial, tribulation, and challenge. That is when you find out what your weaknesses are so that you can build them up. There's nothing wrong with having weaknesses; we all have them. Nobody's perfect. But we are all genetically accurate, and by that I mean that we are all designed to succeed. But we are not perfect.

One of the first Commandments God gave was: "Be fruitful and multiply." Multiplication in life — whether it is to grow a family or to grow money — is a natural desire. But it does not happen easily. You have to follow a certain course, and you're going to have trials and tribulations. You need to accept those as par for the course. Instead of running from them, do the best you can to embrace them and understand them, and know that they too will pass.

Do you know the old saying, "Joy comes in the morning"? It is a season. You are going to go through seasons where it seems like nothing can go wrong and then you're going to go through seasons where it seems like nothing can go right. But they are all just seasons and they are all just part of the process.

How can we truly enjoy success and truly embrace a victory if we have never tasted defeat? You can't have one without the other. Some people can take the simple act of breathing for granted. But someone who has asthma or bronchitis does not take a clear breath for granted.

One thing that helps us to cherish things in our lives and those moments of achieving something great — big or small, financial or any other area of life — is understanding the hard work that it took to get there. The trials and tribulations. The long hours. The sweat. What it took to get there.

When you look at the things that are happening in your life and you think, "Life has dealt me a bad hand. Look at all of these things. They must be omens," they're not omens. They may be signs that you're on the right path, because now you're being challenged. I believe that if things are really easy, there must be a set-up somewhere, because that is just not how life works. You are always going to be challenged and tested. Life is not going to roll out the red carpet for you and say, "This is your dream. Come on and get it."

Fantasizing, Actualizing, Realizing

Let's go back and look at our acronym, FAR: fantasizing, actualizing, and realizing. Let's take a moment right now to fantasize.

There is nothing wrong with fantasizing. Some of the greatest things humankind has accomplished have come out of someone's fantasy. Somebody might have had a fantasy of going to the moon, having cars, being able to communicate on phones that have no wires, being able to connect millions of computers around the world to one another, being able to type in words and hit a button and have the message instantly pop up on somebody else's computer thousands of miles away. Some of the greatest inventions, ideas, and successes are born from fantasies. Some of the best video games that are being sold on the market come from people's fantasies. It is okay to fantasize.

Go back to those childhood days when you fantasized and played cops and robbers, Ken and Barbie, or cowboys and Indians. Maybe you played sports. Maybe you played football in the field with your friends, and somebody was a John Elway and somebody was an Emmit Smith. You had fantasies. It is okay to fantasize. That is one part of your childhood that you don't want to lose. But you don't want to fantasize and leave it at that. You need to go further than that, otherwise you become just a daydreamer.

What is one of your greatest fantasies? Be outrageous. How much money would you like to make? What places do you want to travel? What kind of lifestyle do you want to live? What kind of family would you like to have? What kind of relationships would you like to build?

Be as outrageous as you want to be, but get a very clear picture of what one of your greatest fantasies is. Be very specific. In fact, pull out a pencil and paper and write down what your fantasy is. Be as specific and as detailed as possible. What does it look like? Maybe it is a new car you would like to buy. Maybe you want a new Rolls Royce, BMW, Mercedes, Lexus, or Hummer. It could be anything.

Let's say you want a new BMW M-5. What does it look like? If you're not too sure what it looks like, get a catalog. Go to the BMW web site and print pictures of it. Put the wallpaper on your computer. Print out a picture and keep it in your wallet. You need to develop a dream book of what your fantasies are. A dream book is a book — big or small — that has pictures that represent or symbolize the various goals that you would like to accomplish. It might be a picture of a happy family that is symbolic of the happy family that you would like to have. Maybe it is a picture of the big house that represents a big house you would like to build. Maybe it is a picture of the exact car that you would like. Maybe it is a picture of a vacation spot where you would like to vacation with your friends and family.

You need to be very clear on what that fantasy is. What does it feel like? Granted, you might not have experienced it yet, so you might not know what it feels like. But what do you imagine it feels like?

I want you to close your eyes right now. Think of that BMW M-5 or whatever it is and touch it. I want you to experience it. I want you to inhale very deeply. What does that smell like to you? If it's a new car, smell that new-car smell. What does it feel like? Touch the steering wheel. If it's the beaches of your vacation spot, feel the sand between your toes and on your hands; lie down in it. I want you to wallow around in the sand. What does it feel like?

Get in touch with that fantasy. Fully engage yourself in that experience. What would it mean to you, to your family, and to your business to have that experience? Why must you experience that one particular fantasy? What does it mean to you? What does it mean to your family? What does it mean to your business? I want you to get that clear. Write that down. Why must you experience this fantasy?

What does it mean if you don't experience this fantasy? What is it going to mean to your family if you don't experience this? Write down as many reasons as you can think of why you *must* experience this. Write down what it would mean if you *don't* experience this. You really need to get in touch with the "must" part of it.

Now we need to actualize. Actualization is the process of acting. One definition of actualization is to realize an action or make real. It is the process of determining precisely what you must do to get something done. This is the part where your fantasy starts to become a reality. What do you need to do to have your fantasy transformed into reality?

Before you start thinking of all of the huge and dramatic things that you may have to do, let me ask you something: Have you ever heard of "the butterfly effect"? It was a phrase coined by Edward Lorenz, who was a scientist at MIT. The term "butterfly effect" is used to explain how small changes in initial conditions can change the outcomes of larger patterns. It goes along the same lines as the idea that a one-quarter turn in the stern of a ship can turn the ship off course for miles. One small change can have a huge, dramatic impact on the outcome in your life.

You know who John Travolta is, right? Many of us probably remember him from *Grease* with Olivia Newton-John. That was one of the best films he had done up to that point. Many probably remember him from

Pulp Fiction, which was considered to be his comeback film. He was in that with Samuel L. Jackson.

Now ask yourself: Was that John Travolta's butterfly effect? Was that one movie the thing that set a course for this whole blaze of events that put John Travolta in the top bracket of money earners? He is very popular. He has starred in many movies. He comes back from *Welcome Back, Kotter* and *Grease* to do several of the finest films of our time. Was it really that one movie that did it for him? Was it the film director Quentin Tarantino? Or was it *Pulp Fiction*? Or was it none of those? Was it the stroke of a pen? Was it the initial thought of somebody who thought of the story?

One very specific and small thing can set in motion a chain of events that has made hundreds of millions of dollars in Hollywood and set up the fabulous careers of two actors: Samuel L. Jackson and John Travolta. That's just an example of how very small things can have dramatic effects. Ask yourself what are some of the small things that you can change. They don't have to be huge, dramatic things.

If you're trying to lose weight, you don't have to make sweeping changes to your dietary program and exercise routine. Maybe you get on the bike for 15 minutes. Maybe you cut back on some of the sugars, fats, and carbohydrates — slowly but surely. But do it in such a way that you will be able to stick with it. If you think about it, a very small change can set off huge changes in your life.

Think about not only the big things that you can change, but also some of the small things you can change that can energize you. Maybe you drink a lot of soft drinks and you don't drink enough water. Maybe drinking more water will energize you. Maybe if you started to drink more water, your energy levels would increase. With that change in energy levels, you may feel a little bit more active. With that feeling of being more active, you start to engage in more activities. Those activities start to burn more calories and more body fat. With those increased calories and body fat you're burning, you start to lose weight and your body composition starts to change. You start to notice that you're not so soft and flabby, and you're starting to firm up around your waistline, biceps, chest, and thighs. You're starting to see these changes in your body composition, or on the scale. That starts to give you momentum. That starts to build your confidence.

What did it start with? It all started with drinking more and more water and cutting back on some of the sugary drinks or the other beverages you were drinking. That is an example of how you can make very small changes and see a chain of events start to take place as a result of those small changes.

Here's the thing: You are not far from becoming what it is you are not. You need to understand and accept that. You are just one idea away, one breakthrough away. You are just one patient day away from being able to experience that metamorphosis like the caterpillar does and become that big, beautiful butterfly. You have it in you, just like the caterpillar has it in him to become the butterfly.

You have it in you to become what it is you want to become, to be what it is you want to be. But you need to allow yourself to go through the process of transformation. Don't paralyze the process by trying to be something you're not. Don't cannibalize your future by doing things today that damage your future.

Many people who don't know the process may look at a caterpillar and not see that one day it will fly. There may be people in your life who look at you and think you'll become nothing. They don't understand the butterfly that is inside of you. They don't understand that you have wings that are waiting to come forth, and that you are going to go through this transformation, this metamorphosis, and be reborn as a big, beautiful butterfly. They don't understand that you are going to soar to places that you couldn't reach in your current state as the caterpillar.

You are not far from becoming what it is that you're not. You have it in you. You have that butterfly in you. Allow it to come forth. Remember: you are not far from becoming what you are not. Fantasize about it and then actualize it. When you actualize it and you start to act, you start to make real those fantasies, and that is the realization. You then move your fantasy into reality. Inside of you is a big, beautiful butterfly. Many people may not see it, but that's okay, as long as you know it.

Just because someone looks at a caterpillar and doesn't see the butterfly that's inside, does that mean there is no butterfly? Does their belief that it is only a caterpillar make the reality that there's a butterfly inside not true? Of course not.

People's ideas and beliefs about who you are, what you are, and who you can become have nothing to do with reality. Don't make their beliefs and their reality your own reality. You are genetically accurate. You are engineered for success, and inside of you is a beautiful butterfly waiting to come forth. But you have to have the patience to allow that process to take place, so you experience that transformation.

Don't let the people around you shift and change your reality. Don't let them do it. You have a butterfly in you, and you're not far from becoming what you're not. So allow that butterfly to come forth.

Cash Flow

How does cash really flow? Companies want cash flow. We, as individuals, want cash flow. Everybody wants cash flow. There is nothing wrong with that. But the question is: How can we have more cash flow to us? It's not necessarily about having less cash flow to somebody else; it's about trying to have more cash flow to us. Since the beginning of mankind, the secret of cash flow has been hidden right in the center of the problem-solution model.

What do I mean by that? People will always pursue the business, the individual, or whoever is able to solve their most immediate, pressing problems. Doesn't that make sense? Think about it. If you were sick, whom would you go see? You don't go see the baker. You go to see the doctor, correct? If you were having some sort of legal issue, whom would you go see? You don't go see your personal trainer. You go see your lawyer, right? Now what if you need a mortgage? You go see a mortgage broker or a banker. You don't go down to the local pizza joint unless that's where you're going to have a meeting with a mortgage broker.

The key to being pursued and chased and being the most wanted and the most sought-after person in your business, your marketplace, or your company, and having people throw their money at you, is to have the ability to identify a pressing problem that people have and to provide a solid solution. It is that simple. People have problems; they want solutions. What kind of problem do the people at your company have? Or, if you run your own business, what kind of problem does your market have, and what kind of solution do you offer that will cause people to pursue you?

You have to ask why people would pursue you. Why should people give you their money? It's not because you have something to sell; that doesn't make a difference. People have products to sell all day long. Just because you have something to sell doesn't mean people want to buy it. If you do have something to sell that's kind of dorky and your family is buying it, they are buying it because they love you. Let's be real: People don't buy something just because somebody is selling it. People buy things to solve some sort of problem they have. It can be a serious problem or a minor problem. It can be a problem or need of entertainment, or it can be one of finances.

The bottom line is this: You need to be able to solve a problem in the company that you work for or in your marketplace in such a unique way that your company is willing to give you the raise you're working towards or people are willing to give you the money instead of giving the money to your competition. You have to create a desire and need for *your* solution as opposed to somebody else's.

A person who wants a hamburger can go to Burger King, Wendy's, or anyplace. They can make one at home if they want to. But a person who wants a Big Mac can only go to McDonald's. What specific solution can you offer to a specific desire, craving, or need that people who are experiencing problems want? People have to crave it; they have to have an appetite for it. Let's get really specific here.

At a seminar someone said: "Tell me what you want in your business and I will give you whatever you want or as much business as you want." We went around the room and people said that they wanted the best location or other things. "Give me this" and "Give me that." After they were finished with their requests, he said, "I'll give you all of that." But all he wanted was a starving crowd. He wanted people whose problems he could solve. I totally agree with that. But nowadays I think that it has to go a step further. You need more than a starving crowd; you need to have a starving crowd that has an appetite and craving for what you specifically offer.

It's very simple. You can have a crowd of hungry people. You can have a rack of ribs stacked sky-high, dripping with sauce. You think you're going to rack up sales with this rack of spare ribs. But then you find out that the starving people are die-hard vegetarians with carrot juice pumping through their veins. You have got a problem. You've got a hungry crowd, but they don't crave spare ribs. They crave celery sticks, lettuce, and tofu. You got what you wanted — a starving crowd. But you were not specific enough. You have meat, but your hungry crowd is vegetarian. The point is this: You need to solve very specific problems for very specific people. That's it.

If you work for a company, identify problems that have gone unresolved — very specific problems — and find out a way to solve those problems. That is going to immediately raise your level of contribution and your value to the company. That helps to accelerate you through the ranks of your company to get raises and become overqualified for your current position. If you run a business, you want to identify and know the specific problem of your marketplace. Be very specific. You want to know what that problem is, and you want to provide the solution.

Cash Flow

Over-Deliver

Here is the big one: You need to make reality greater than the promise. Write that down because it's very important. If you over-deliver, you can almost immediately find yourself in the top 1% of income earners and companies in this country. You need to make reality greater than the promise.

Many companies out there advertise this, that, and the other. People put all of kinds great things on their résumés. They get hired or somebody retains their services or buys their products, and they under-perform or the product under-performs. The person who purchased the product is feeling a little bit cheated. You did not make the reality bigger than the promise.

Even if you sell yourself like crazy, your objective is always to make sure that all of those big promises that you're making are still nothing compared to the impact of what it is you can give to them in reality. Do you know what happens when you do that? People don't come to you only once to get a problem solved, they come to you over and over again. If you run any kind of company, you know that it is really important for people to come to you again and again, because having people buy from you only once will put a little money in your pocket, but it is not going to create wealth.

You will create wealth in your company by having those people come back to you over and over again with such an overwhelmingly high level of satisfaction that they burst at the seams wanting to give you money for solutions to new or ongoing problems that they have for which they feel you have the most satisfying permanent or temporary solution. They will also start to send other people to you.

This whole process of cash flow is wrapped up in: "What is the problem?" and "Here is the solution." That's it. Define problems. Present solutions of your own or present solutions as a third-party for somebody else. In other words, you can be the go-between, the broker of the deal. But there's one thing that stands true: If you solve small problems, you will make small money. If you solve big problems, you will make big money.

One of the biggest problems you can solve for somebody is a financial problem. That's why everything associated with investing and making money — seminars, audio programs, videos, books, and e-books — has a higher price tag than products relating to most other topics. A book on how to get weeds out of your garden or how to make light and fluffy muffins does solve a person's problem, but it does not command the same price as a book or program on how to make money in stocks.

Getting the weeds out of someone's garden or perfecting a muffin recipe solves the end user's problem. However, solving the problem of making money in stocks solves a bigger problem than the weed or the muffin problem, and, more important, the end result of solving that problem means more money for the end user.

The size of the problem you solve impacts the amount of wealth that you can build from that problem-solution model. You need to understand supply and demand. Where there is huge demand and small supply, the price of the supply can increase.

How about finding a problem that needs a solution? There may be many solutions available, but maybe there is no satisfactory solution. If you come out with a killer solution, a solution that just *works*, the demand for that solution can go up. Because you're the only one with the solution, the supply becomes very limited, and you're able to raise the price of that solution and make more money per unit that you sell.

How does cash flow? It is very simple. Cash flows to those who are able to solve other people's pressing problems. Write that down. In fact, write that on an index card and to tape it on your wall or your bathroom mirror so the understanding of how cash flows is always in front of you.

If you're not making enough money, you are not solving enough problems for people. Or, the problems that you're solving are too small. Don't simply ask for more money, look to solve more or bigger problems. Then the money automatically follows.

Identify more problems and solve more problems. Guess what? Your pockets are going to start being lined with money. They are going to burst at the seams. Wealth will be yours.

People who solve problems for people are money magnets. They can't stop the money from coming at them. They couldn't stop it if they wanted to. They will die, and the money will still be flowing in their direction. The empire that they built was won around the whole problem-solution model and the money continues to flow their way.

Let's do an exercise. Do an inventory of yourself or your company. Identify what problems you are solving for people — not what problems you think you are solving, but what problems you are actually solving. Be honest with yourself or else this exercise will do you no good.

Now, look at how much revenue you're bringing in — whether you're working for somebody or you operate your own company. Ask yourself if you are really solving those problems for those people. Just look at the revenue. Are the problems you're solving for people very small problems, so you have small revenue? Or are you solving big problems for people, but just not solving enough of them?

You need to identify what problems you are solving for people. Then you need to identify what problems you *can* solve for people. If you do a little investigative work, you will find a whole lot of problems that people need to have solved. You don't need to create problems for people that you can then solve. There are plenty of problems already out there. This world is teeming with problems and people begging for someone to provide solutions. That is how to get people to give you money. Don't beg, plead, or cajole.

When you have a headache, what you do? Do you reach for a pop? Maybe you do. Most people go to the store and they buy aspirin, Advil, or Excedrin or some other brand of pain reliever. They are buying it as a solution to the problem of a throbbing pain pounding in their head. Are they buying it because they think the bottle is sexy? There may be some people who do that, but probably not. They are buying it as a solution to the problem that they have, and the problem is a headache. They see that that pill and that bottle are a solution.

When you solve problems for people, you have to answer the question of what is in it for them. But if you build your model, your life, around solving problems for people, then the question of "what is in it for me?" is already answered. You've already taken care of a certain amount of resistance to your offer. You're coming to them from the position of a solution to an existing, pressing problem that they would like to see resolved. Your solution is going to take them closer to where they want to be, or move them further away from where they don't want to be.

Have you ever gone to the store and purchased a pain reliever like aspirin for a headache? Chances are you have.

When you got home and took the aspirin and the headache went away, did you ever go back to the store, slam down the bottle on the counter, and say, "Give me my money back"? Did you ever go back and ask for a refund on a bottle of Excedrin or Advil? Of course you didn't.

The chances of a person having "buyer's remorse" after a problem has been solved for them are very slim.

One way to simultaneously satisfy a huge number of clients or customers — or the company that you work for — is to make sure that whatever you do is always solving a problem that already exists. People will celebrate you with raises, promotions, and recognition.

Your lifestyle can change if you understand that this whole thing about creating wealth — this whole thing about having cash flow in your direction — is all wrapped up in understanding that people will give their money to those who are able to solve their most pressing problems.

It's not because it is a cool product or a ground-floor opportunity, or because the company said this industry is booming. It's not because it sells literature or because you're excited about it, but because it solves a real problem that is causing people pain that they want to have relieved. That is how you create wealth. That is how you get cash to flow to you. It's really that simple.

If you want cash to flow to you, don't go begging for it. Don't try to scam people out of it or try to sell them things that may be worthless to them. Find out what people really need. Find out what causes people pain and be a reliever of that pain. Be a healer. Be a solution provider. Guess what? The money is going to be unlocked and is going to flow right to you. That's how it works. Ask any company — big or small — what their revenue drivers are. It's going to be their products that are solving problems for people. Whether they are selling to businesses or to individuals, they are solving problems on one level or another. They may be solving an individual's entertainment "problem" or some kind of big corporate network problem.

Sometimes people purchase products or services not to solve an existing problem, but to avoid getting a problem. Why do you think people get alarm systems? They don't want to have the theft problem, or they want to be able to solve the theft problem when it happens. Why do people buy firewalls for their computers? They want to prevent hacker problems. It still goes right back to people having problems and people looking for solutions, even if it's solutions to potential problems.

You want to know how cash flows. The number one reason why people pay you cash right here, right now, with a smile, and willingly is because you can solve their most immediate, pressing problem. You can take away the pain they are experiencing or you can provide the pleasure that they want to move towards as fast as possible. That is how cash flows.

Secrets to Creating Wealth

72

Sowing and Reaping

There's an East Indian proverb: "If you sow a thought, you reap an act. If you sow an act, you reap a habit. If you sow a habit, you reap your character. If you sow your character, you reap a destiny." You may have heard that before, but the most powerful part of that is the idea of sowing. Whatever it is you have right now, that's the most it will ever be. But when you give something away, that's the least it's ever going to be.

Let's use a farmer as an example. A farmer knows that whatever seeds he has on hand are the most they're ever going to be until he sows them. He knows the moment he sows them, that's the least they're ever going to be. Once they are sown, they have the opportunity to grow. But growth doesn't happen instantly. In the sowing and reaping process, a farmer knows that he will be rewarded for his patience.

You need to understand that you will be rewarded for your patience after you sow. If you are working on your lawn, you don't lay down your seeds and fertilizer, water the grass, plop yourself on your stairs, and stare at the grass waiting for it to grow, do you? That doesn't make any sense. It needs time to grow. It needs some time for the nutrients you put in it to take effect. It needs to continue to be watered and nurtured, and then you're going to see it grow. Then it's going to become plush, beautiful, green grass, right? When a farmer plants and plows, he understands that he has his season of sowing and he has his season of reaping.

That's how it is with life. It's one of those powerful principles and spiritual laws that is an absolute truth, like the law of gravity. The law of gravity says that if you jump off of a building, you will hit the ground, right? The law of reaping and sowing says that you reap what you sow.

A really good way to teach children how to sow —and it's good for adults also — is to get a Chia Pet.

Chia Pets are very simple and inexpensive, and they provide a quick lesson in sowing and reaping. All you have to do is follow very simple steps. You prepare the Chia Pet, put the seeds on it, and fill it up with water; this is the sowing process. In just a few days, you start to see sprouts growing on your Chia Pet.

That's basically how the sowing and reaping process works. You prepare the soil, plant your seeds, water it, and then give it the time it needs to sprout and spring forth in your life the rewards for actually going through that sowing process. If you have a garden, then you definitely know about the benefits of being patient after you've sown something.

You also know the rewards of reaping something. We have our own garden. It's an incredible thing; I constantly go and look at the garden, at the parts of the plants growing. I look at the cucumbers, eggplants, bell peppers, and jalapeño peppers. It's just an exciting process, and I look forward to putting the vegetables into a nice, green, leafy salad.

It's exciting to start to reap from your efforts of sowing. But there's something else that's also fascinating. You can plant, for example, a papaya or even a watermelon seed and when you reap that harvest, there are multiple seeds. Sometimes there are hundreds or even thousands of seeds. You started with just one.

There are many different things that you can sow: your money, your time, your wisdom, your knowledge, and your understanding. But whatever you sow, you will always have a time to reap what you sow.

You also have to be aware of where you sow. You may be struggling, saying, "I am sowing. I'm working and I'm trying. I'm doing this and that." Maybe you are. But *where* are you sowing? That's important. A farmer can sow and plough a desert all day long, but what are his chances of reaping a harvest if he is sowing in the desert? You need to look at where you are sowing your money and where you are sowing your time.

For the most part, we reap whatever it is we sow our time into. For example, if you have an employer, you go to your job and you sow an hour and you reap an hourly wage or some kind of compensation. Even when you sow your time to watch a comedy on television, you reap entertainment. Oftentimes, a joke that is delivered in a few seconds can keep you laughing for minutes, hours, or even days as you go back and reflect on it.

The law of reaping and sowing is just as real as the law of gravity. You need to take control of what you sow today, because that will allow you to control what you reap tomorrow.

Success Routine

Desire is important in planning to achieve your goals, but equally if not more important are your habits that move you either closer to your dreams and goals or further away from your dreams and goals. You need to set up a daily success routine. By routine, I don't mean something that is boring. It is fun, energetic, engaging, and active. It is something that can be measured. It can move you closer to your objectives.

Think of it as a checklist like a pilot goes through before take-off. On a day-to-day basis, you need to have what is called a "preflight routine," if you will. This ensures that all systems are go, and that you are moving closer to your objectives every day by achieving the smaller goals and objectives that have an impact on your larger goals and objectives.

Let me share with you what our personal daily routine looks like. Your daily routine does not have to be the same as ours. But our example will help you understand that what we do, we do habitually and it moves us closer to what we are looking to achieve. Monday through Friday, I rise at 4:30 in the morning. On Saturday and Sunday I'm up at around 6:30 or maybe 7:30. After I get up and brush my teeth, the first thing I do is pray and read my Bible. I put on some very nice meditative music, sometimes it is praise music and sometimes it is environmental sounds. I meditate until about 5:30 a.m.

At 5:30 a.m. I check e-mail. I don't check e-mail before dawn when I am praying and meditating and reading my Bible, because there is so much e-mail in there that I will get distracted. The next thing you know, I spend more time checking e-mail than I really wanted to spend and my whole day is thrown off. I really like to jumpstart my day with prayer, reading my Bible, and meditating — getting really relaxed, focused, comfortable, and in tune with God and myself. I get that early rhythm going before I get started into the actual work.

At about 6:00 a.m., I check the markets to see what happened overnight, because we have companies and products that deal with investing and trading. I check the Dow Jones and the NASDAQ. I look at some of the currencies. At 6:30, it is time to work out. I work out at home or at the gym. Sometimes it is really hard to pull away from the computer, because maybe I didn't finish checking all the e-mail or I wanted to check a chart on something, but I've developed a discipline.

It is 6:30 a.m.; it is time to go work out. If I don't get up from my desk and go to work out at 6:30, do you know what is going to happen? Nothing. I'm going to give an excuse like, "Well, I worked out yesterday and my body needs a day off anyway so I'll just go work out tomorrow." That is not what I need. That is breaking the pattern and starting to defer to a bad habit; it is being inconsistent. What I need to do is remain in control and say that it's time to get up and go work out from 6:30 to 7:15 a.m. The amount of time I spend working out is flexible because it depends on if I'm only lifting weights or if I'm lifting weights and doing some light cardio or only doing cardio. My shortest sessions are ones where I'm only doing cardio, because I'll do 25 minutes of high-intensity cardio.

After I am finished working out, I will take a shower and start reading. The exact time I do these various things is flexible, but the objective is for me to be at my desk at 7:45 so that I can start to read. I play very soft music in the background in my headphones while I am reading. The music helps my mind to relax and keeps it receptive and focused on what I am reading. That is the early reading session.

I like to read until about 9:30 in the morning. Then I go back to finish checking e-mail. After that, I start to prepare for the trading session. The markets open up at about 9:30 a.m. I look for the S&P to open and get ready to chart that. From the time the markets open, my day is filled with working on various projects, checking in on some of our other businesses, checking in on marketing stats, putting together new campaigns, endorsements, and joint venture deals, doing new product creations and doing a lot of data mining with our clients.

My workday begins, and within that time frame there are very specific tasks that get done. How far you go with your routine depends on what your objectives are and what you're going to be doing through-out that day. Maybe you have a job that you work, so you have to put in time for things that you do for your job, for your employer. Then, when you come home, you start to take care of the adjustments neces-sary to achieve your personal goals.

You will never achieve anything significant in your life without the involvement of other people. We have client meetings and we have staff meetings. We go over specific things for ongoing projects. We make sure that all the tasks get done and everybody is accountable for his or her part of the process.

Don't try to go it alone, regardless of how sure you are of yourself and regardless of how confident you are of yourself. Don't get so cocky as to think you can do it all by yourself. It is not all about you. It is about you and other people working together.

You will never, ever achieve anything significant without the involvement of other people. Throughout the day I also listen to vari-ous CDs and tapes: instrumental, seminars, motivational recordings, and marketing programs. I like to keep that learning process going constantly so I am constantly feeding my mind. Remember the Third Influence? I am constantly feeding my mind with all kinds of information to get that positive, deliberate Third Influence in my life to help me move closer to my objectives. Nobody's perfect, and nobody knows everything. If you think you know everything, you're probably going to have a huge collapse in your life.

I keep myself teachable; always ready to learn. I keep myself in this learning state so, regardless of what accomplishments I may have achieved, experienced and enjoyed, I know that there is always a higher level and that there is more to be achieved.

I know it is going to require more information to get to that level. It will require more of me, it will require stretching myself further. If I don't currently have the skill set that I need to get to that next level then somebody else has it. I need to find out who has it and go get it from them. In many cases, that means either having my own personal coach, which I do have, or listening to tapes, reading books, or watching videos. I encourage you to do the same thing. Remember, the Third Influence in your life is extremely powerful.

Depending on the time of day I finish up with work, my wife and I will have movie time. We will rent movies, especially on Tuesdays because that is when the new movies come out at Blockbuster and Hollywood Video. Usually movie night is also sushi night. We watch a movie or two and have sushi.

Sometimes we play tennis, get out of the house, get some nice good exercise, get the heart pumping; it helps to add a lot of spice to our lives. Sometimes we go to the movies or we go fishing. We make time to go out and do things — some are planned, some are spontaneous. But the thing is we make sure that we incorporate activities into our days that are fun because we do work a lot.

We don't have a problem with working a lot; it is really a lot of fun. But you need to have variety, too.

We enjoy what we are doing and we hope that you enjoy what you are doing. If you are not enjoying it, I hope and pray that you are moving towards the area of your life that you are doing what you enjoy. Then the work is not even going to matter. You are really going to enjoy the process.

After doing the market wrap-ups in the evenings, or doing any videos for our trading services (we do multimedia video analysis for our trading services, which are done in the evening after the market closes), I will pull away from the desk, go upstairs, and put up my feet in this really comfortable chair in the bedroom. I won't take any phone calls unless it is absolutely urgent. I love it when my wife brings me a freshly made fruit smoothie. I am really addicted to her fruit smoothies. Then I turn on the television and see if there's anything on that I want to watch. If there's nothing on that I really want to watch — if there's not an interesting episode of Hardball or The O'Reilly Factor — if there's nothing really engaging, entertaining, or informative going on there, I open up another book.

It doesn't matter whether or not I read at that time, because I always like to read before I go to bed. They say that reading for 30 minutes before you go to bed allows the information to basically marinate in your mind while you're sleeping. I am a true believer in that, as I said when we talked earlier about the Third Influence. We talked about playing audio programs while you sleep, but it is also good to read before you go to sleep. I like to read certain books before I go to sleep.

Make sure that your lifestyle is aligned with what you want to achieve on a day-to-day basis. Success is not about dividing and conquering, it is about adding and multiplying. In everything that you do, look to add value to other people's lives and to multiply your wealth by adding that value to other people's lives. You can't do that if you don't take care of yourself. Methodically plan and deliberately take the actions necessary to add value to people's lives.

Figure out how to add massive value into people's lives and you will automatically begin to multiply your wealth. Take care of yourself and, starting today, put together your own success routine.

I hope that you really enjoyed this short journey that we've taken together in the *Secrets of Creating Wealth*. These are discoveries that had a true impact on my life, and I know they work. This isn't theoretical.

These are the things that took me up from the depths of poverty, homelessness, and bankruptcy and have allowed my family and I to enjoy a very comfortable, healthy, and wealthy lifestyle. I battled many different things along the way.

We didn't cover everything here, but we covered more than enough for you to understand that regardless of where you are in your life, what your current financial condition is, what your current assets are, and what people may think or say about you, you have the ability to make a significant impact on people's lives and experience the wealth of your dreams.

I'd like to leave you with several key points to remember. You may be a caterpillar now, but that butterfly is inside of you. Allow that transformation to happen. Pay attention to the Third Influence in your life. It has a significant impact on your destiny.

Remember that habit is significantly more powerful than desire. You can have all of the desires in the world, but you need to develop the habit to support those desires and move you closer to achieving your objectives.

You are not far from becoming what you are not. FAR is an acronym for Fantasizing, Actualizing, and Realizing. Engage your fantasy and then actualize the process. Lay out the plan, put together the blueprint, and take the action consistently, congruently, and daily to transform those

Secrets to Creating Wealth

fantasies into reality. You have to act consistently, congruently, and daily if you want to realize those fantasies.

Remember that money flows to those who solve problems for other people. It is not about how much money you need to pay your bills or to impress other people. It is not about how famous you want to become. If you want to become a money magnet and a well of wealth, you need to identify what people's problems are and create solutions for them. Then you need to deliver or facilitate the delivery of those solutions to those people.

Remember that it is more blessed to give than it is to receive. Remember to practice reaping and sowing. When you give, you receive a return multiplied a hundredfold or a thousand fold. It is fun to get things, but the giver is the most blessed because he will get the multiplied returns.

In your service to others make the reality greater than the promise. The leaders in this world are those who over-deliver. If you want to be in the top 1% of your chosen field, have a successful business, or have a fulfilling life, you have to make the reality greater than the promise. You have to practice the process of over-delivering and exceeding people's expectations every day. You have to carve your space in their hearts as the "go-to" guy or girl, the one person they know will always over-deliver to them.

Success is not about dividing and conquering, beating out your competitors, or beating down other people, it is about adding and multi-plying. When you add value to any place, you become a magnet to other people. They gravitate towards you. One of the greatest values you can add to somebody's life or to any marketplace is to be a solution provider or a solution facilitator. When you add that value, you will automatically begin to multiply your wealth. People will throw their money at you to experience the solution you provide, to be relieved of their pain, or to experience the pleasure that they desire to experience.

May you experience the wealth of your dreams.

CLAIM YOUR FREE BONUS IMMEDIATELY!

www.WealthBuildingVideos.com

Now that you are aware of the basic secrets to creating wealth, it's time to begin experience building wealth yourself.

I encourage you to visit www.WealthBuildingVideos.com immediately to claim your free bonus with your purchase of this book.

Among its many benefits, you will find.

- ◆ Online video coaching from me personally to help you transform your life and experience wealth and abundance.

- ◆ Information on ways to share Secrets of Creating Wealth with your family, friends, associates and co-workers.

- ◆ PowerPoint presentations you can use to teach the Secrets of Creating Wealth principles, concepts and ideas to your company, Church groups, adult learning classes or in your own seminars.

- ◆ Ways to connect with other Secrets of Creating Wealth readers from around the world.

- ◆ Ways to connect and interact with me and my team of Wealth Coaches.

www.WealthBuildingVideos.com

Discover The "Behind-The-Scenes" Mastermind Session That Created This Book

Blam! The Shot Rang-Out. I Fell To The Ground.

Laying There Bleeding, I Knew It Was Time For A Change… Five Years Later, I Was Running A Multi-Million-Dollar Business And Making Six Figures A Month Having Fun Working From Home.

My methodology is so simple, it's embarrassing. And I've already taught hundreds of others in my sold-out $1,000.00 a month coaching club to follow my path to wealth and fulfillment.

Now I BOLDLY ASSERT I can quickly teach my simple secrets to YOU… instantly programming your life for success, converting your dreams to reality, eliminating the factors holding you back from a lifetime of accomplishment, and launching a bullet proof path for accumulating wealth!

And best of all, you can be on your way to unstoppable confidence and achievement in under an hour for a fraction of what anyone has had to pay for access to these secrets.

If you have been reading self-help books, going to seminars, and doing all the "right things" but success has still eluded you,

it is probably not your fault. It's simply because you never learned the *Secrets of Creating Wealth* or discovered the amazing "Power of the Third Influence."

I still remember being young and dumb and getting evicted from my apartment and cast out on the mean streets of D.C... Using up all my chances in school until I was booted out the door during the tenth grade... Hooked up with the wrong crowd and ended up on the business end of a Saturday Night Special... And to this day, I carry the bullet in my leg as a reminder.

Today, my family runs an endless empire of online businesses, offline businesses, and three different coaching clubs. I am known as one of the powerhouses of the Internet and teach others to replicate our success.

I'm Not Trying to Impress You... I Just Want You to See YOU Can Have This Same Kind of Life Yourself!

You are engineered for success. You can't help it. It's in your genes. **It's just that no one ever gave you a roadmap**. Imagine how successful your life could be *one year from today* if you had a plan of action.

All you need are the keys to success. They aren't a secret. And they're so simple, it will blow your mind. But I'll bet nobody ever told them to you. (I know nobody told them to me).

But I want you to avoid the struggles I faced to get where I am today. No, I INSIST on helping you. What would you do if you knew beyond the shadow of a doubt that you COULD BE SUCCESSFUL? That you could...

◆ Drive whatever kind of car you choose;

◆ Live in your dream home in the finest neighborhood;

Secrets to Creating Wealth

◆ Dine at gourmet restaurants without a reservation;

◆ Visit tropical paradises or culture-rich cities at the drop of a hat;

◆ Give expensive gifts to your family without looking at the price tag.

If you could get all that, would you give what I have to say a chance? Because I'm being straight with you. Just a few years ago, I couldn't imagine living the life I live today. Let me assure — all of it is possible.

You simply need someone to tell you what to do.

Some people say I've been blessed with the Midas touch. But it wasn't always this way. As you can imagine, doors don't automatically open for ghetto drop-outs. But there's no doubt I was missing...

The Keys To Success

I drifted from failure to failure, always looking for the easy way out. I used to buy all those big $20 books on how to make money with get rich quick schemes. Some of those ideas were just dumb.

There was the arbitration business, vinyl repair service, and vending machine route, but nothing worked. But the reason they didn't work was because I didn't put in any effort. I didn't even bother to read the manuals.

I expected fame and fortune were going to drop down out of the sky. It didn't. I expected checks were going to magically appear without any effort. They didn't.

When I realized it would take more than being positive, saying my affirmations and being hopeful, I did indeed put forth what I thought was some sincerely serious effort... yet things still didn't turn around.

Now please realize, just like you I did not have an overwhelming desire to be a failure, to file bankruptcy, to be evicted, to take all I own to pawnshops and live shamefully broke. There was something missing…

"Wealth is your birthright! And Stephen Pierce shows you exactly what it takes to claim the personal and financial success that should be rightfully yours. Stephen's story will inspire and motivate you. His wealth building strategies have made him rich and they can work for you too."

~Will Bonner~
Director, Agora Learning Institute

The Simple Path From Failure To Success

The path to the top started with baby steps. I read Napoleon Hill's *Think and Grow Rich*, W. Clement Stone's *Greatest Success Secret*, and Norman Vincent Peale's *Power of Positive Thinking*. Actually, I didn't just read them; I devoured them.

No starving man ever appreciated a meal more than I valued these books. All of a sudden, things didn't seem so bad. After years of stumbling blindly in the dark, I found the path leading to success. Today, as the coach to hundreds in my high priced programs, I shortcut their learning curve.

I began to look at my fumbles and bumbles in a new light — as part of a learning curve which was now accelerating rapidly. I even discovered my impressive strength amidst the failures, which I now aimed squarely at the top. I sharpened my focus and blasted off.

"Stephen Pierce is a perfect example of someone who doesn't just learn what everyone else learns, he applies what everyone else doesn't. His Wealth CD's will show anyone who is serious about really making it financially, how to do it. If you are one of those people who is looking to make it big by winning the lottery, this is NOT for you.

However, if you are prepared to listen and follow the wisdom of a man who has risen from the depths of despair to multimillionaire, get these CD's now!"

~John Assaraf~
New York Times and **Wall Street Journal** Best-Selling Author

Uncovering Hidden Talents

I took a brutally honest inventory of my skills and started my first moves online. I hit a number of singles waiting for the right pitch to blast it out of the park and when I discovered the futures market, I found my niche.

When I got started online, there were very few trading sites. There were some forums and newsgroups but that was it. Nothing really solid. I began studying the market and following the trends. Soon, I caught the rhythm of the futures market and understood the direction of the market.

So many people clamored for my scoop on the futures market, I was forced to throw up my first sites. Then I began emailing my suggested trades and began to build a following. My daily trades were outperforming expensive high paid services when out of the blue, fortune smiled on me. A subscriber wanted to pay me five thousand dollars to teach him my trading methodology. Instead, I started a paid subscription service and charged $350 a month. Within days, I had over one hundred paid subscribers and I was banking, over $35,000 dollars a month! (Today, if I have a month like that I think it's slow!)

My first ebook was Rapid Fire Swing trading which did $49,000 in the first fifty days. To date, I've sold over five thousand copies banking $249,750 from this one product. Thousands of people signed on for my daily market analysis emails. And rave reviews poured in:

"Hi, Stephen. It has been an excellent experience trading your RF Swing Trader. I don't know how you do it, but it is fantastic. Over $3.000.00 in one week with a small account, can't complain! Keep it coming and God bless you and yours."

~Hilario Vieira~
St. Catharines, Canada

"Hello Stephen, This week was the first time that I ever made a Futures Trade and I followed your recommendation for Cotton which gave me a profit of $725 in just 3 days. I am anxious to see what you have to offer in the coming week that can help to add to my profits."

~Paul Shoemaker~
Woody Point, Newfoundland

"Stephen obviously knows what he is doing, look at the results, but on top of having incredible results… he CARES about you as a trader, and a person.(email him a question, and learn for yourself!!) For the price of RFST, it will pay for itself many, many, many times over!!!!"

~Keith Aitken~
Toronto

Those reviews and hundreds more gave me the drive to go even further. Other trading products I've launched made Rapid Fire Swing Trading seem like spare change. Some of these products have made over a million dollars and they continue to sell through my affiliate connections day after day.

But this was just the beginning to becoming what many have said is an…

Overnight Internet Celebrity

The Internet marketing world was filled with distortions, lies, and hype. When I published *The Whole Truth*, it was a breath of fresh air. But I wasn't prepared for the impact that followed.

I revealed some of the most effective marketing techniques and condemned the deceptive ones. Within days, *The Whole Truth* blazed new ground on the Internet and became one of the best selling ebooks of all time. But less than 20 pages of the book created nonstop controversy. In those pages I disclosed a strategy that virtually guaranteed top positions in search engine rankings — the Smart Pages.

Everyone had an opinion about Smart Pages. The mammoth search optimization firms hated them because this $97 product outperformed their outrageously priced services. I was subjected to torrents of abuse and invective because my product performed as promised. In fact, rumors surfaced that Google changed the way they ranked pages because our Smart Pages were making it too easy to rank highly!

And at about that time, I started my Internet Coaching service which is still active today. I've met thousands of Internet entrepreneurs. Many of them were reaching pinnacles of success; others were scrapping the bottom when they started. And I began to turn their failures into towering homeruns.

"NOTHING teaches better than experience and example... and Stephen Pierce gives you BOTH! His Wealth CDs give you practical examples, steps, and tools that make a difference in your life — FAST!

Within the first 5 minutes, Stephen gives you specific strategies you can use to change your DESTINY and they come straight from the depths of his own experiences.. the same experiences he used to transform his life into one of unlimited abundance.

His genuine desire to help you succeed and find your own path to greatness shines through in every minute of this power-packed program! Do yourself and your family a favor, get this program NOW!

~Jim Edwards~
Author, *5 Steps To Getting Anything You Want*

I reached into my bag of tricks for my exclusive coaching clients and shared...

The Power of The Third Influence

It's not another strategy or tactic that builds wealth; it's an iron-clad mindset. It means shedding the failure thinking of the past and locking your compass on your destination and never swerving from the goal. I'll tell you shortly how quickly and easily you can accomplish this. ORDER NOW!

"Stephen Pierce's enthusiasm, zest and message is positively magnetic. With absolutely no advantages and everything against him Stephen shows you how anybody can rise above any obstacle to become successful, wealthy and happy. How? Just follow Stephen's message."

~Yanik Silver~
Internet Marketing Expert, Author of *Public Domain Riches*

Have you ever wondered why so many people have read *Think and Grow Rich* and hundreds of other self-help literature, yet struggle to accomplish their goals? Clearly, these people have "thought" but they haven't grown rich. I'm about to reveal what's been missing.

◆ The inside story of how I went from homeless street-bum to Internet mega-success story and the **simple adjustment you can make for instant results**.

◆ How to get <u>everything</u> you want in life... without... *force, struggle or unethical behavior!* (No need to pull the stunts I did as a kid. Just apply my simple suggestions... and... sit back while the money, fame and fortune seek you out almost effortlessly!)

Learn More Secrets of Creating Wealth

◆ The **single most important thing you must do** before you go out and purchase a single self-help book or audio set. Ignore this and your purchase will just be another book taking up space on your shelf. Follow my advice and you'll pocket endless riches.

◆ How to find out what you really, *really* want! (Not one person in a thousand knows this… yet… it's *crucial* if you want to achieve your dreams with the least amount of time, effort and struggle on your part.)

◆ Why people are programmed for failure. (And… what you absolutely must do instead to **give yourself an "unfair advantage"** when it comes to launching your next effort!)

◆ Why the Power of the Third Influence is the **single most important indicator of your success!** (Most successful businessmen won't share this with outsiders but it's the truth nonetheless.)

◆ A simple way to **eliminate failure thinking**. This simple secret was only known (and used) by my coaching members. Now, they can be in your hands for instant results.

◆ The **real secrets** for making *mind-boggling* amounts of money and achieving your dreams! (Only a handful of people ever reach their goals and those who do *never* share their secrets.)

◆ A simple exercise you can do to *sleep* your way to success! Years later, I still do this exercise every night without fail and continue to increase my wealth… and you can too.

Secrets to Creating Wealth

◆ A quick way **to zap stress out of your life**. No need for years of therapy. Just follow this instant formula for relief.

◆ The "missing link" in most self-help books… or… why most people who try hard to pull themselves up fail in the process. (But once you discover this missing ingredient, your success is guaranteed!)

◆ What a simple high school chemistry experiment reveals about your chances for success. Master this simple lesson and you'll have all the motivation you need to **reach the top and achieve wealth beyond your wildest dreams**.

◆ How to reverse the poverty in your life and stop failure dead in its tracks. **You'll taste the sweetness of wealth** and yesterday's failures will rocket you forward to tomorrow's achievements.

◆ The <u>secret</u> behind Mike Tyson's success and his slide into failure. If he knew the lesson of the Third Influence, he'd still be at the top.

◆ How to recognize the presence of the Third Influence in your life and how you can **harness it so your success can go on autopilot.**

It doesn't matter what you have in your bank account or what your current assets are. I know you can have the breakthroughs you desire and start living a fulfilling life.

Activate the Power of the Third Influence In Your Life

"Stephen Pierce's incredibly powerful strategies and techniques have helped us bring in an additional $173,317 dollars in revenue in the last 5 months. Stephen Pierce is in the top 1% of marketers and entrepreneurs in the world today. Eat every word he says up and immense profits will be your dessert."

Mike Litman
#1 Best-Selling Author of *Conversations*
with Millionaires

Since sharing my success mindset with my coaching members, they've been begging me for a product they could share with their friends and family.

These people — among them the sharpest marketers in the world — have read all the self-help books, bought all the tape sets, and attended all the seminars.

But only after learning about the Power of The Third Influence did everything connect for them.

Up until this point, the ONLY way to discover how to harness the Power of the Third Influence was to be a member of my coaching club and **pay $1,000.00 every month.**

But, I believe in giving back to the community. I tithe 15% of my income to Church and several other organizations worthy of support. Releasing this double CD set to the public is one more way of giving.

Begin to Accumulate Massive Wealth

Look, I know you've probably purchased self-help products before and you're probably wondering "What's so different about the *Secrets of Creating Wealth?*"

The answer is something I've learned from my years of coaching. Many people purchase these products but few apply their concepts.

You see, many of them take months to understand and still longer to put into practice.

Others require almost superhuman effort to achieve their promises.

THREE HOURS OF AMAZING AUDIO!

With me to guide you … you can easily turn your life around and in these THREE HOURS of audio, I will personally help you unlock what's holding you back from creating wealth, and help you transform your life from one of constant money worries, health problems, guilty feelings, fear, procrastination and confusion into a life of financial abundance, vitality, contentment, fulfillment and peace.

These three hours of audio (*available as mp3 downloads*) will sharpen and illuminate your life and move you closer, quickly, to experiencing the wealth you desire… and deserve.

My Problem, Your Bargain

Now most of the people in my coaching program are delighted I am sharing my mental mindset. But others are likely to be a bit upset. I'm not going to charge you what others have paid for this information. No way. **Your cost is just $97 which is about 1% of what the others have paid.**

That is not going to win friends among some of my coaching members so the deal is on for right now. But, I reserve the right to remove this offer at any time.

So you'll want to snag a set of *Secrets of Creating Wealth* while you can. You can take advantage of this special offer by going to:

www. Morgan-James.com/wealthaudio

Prove It To Yourself!

Here's the deal, **just say yes,** and I'll rush a copy of the *Secrets of Wealth* audio to you immediately.

Listen to the set as soon as you get it. Follow the simple action plan. Watch for a change in your attitude followed by a huge change in your financial situation.

Take ~~thirty,~~ ~~sixty,~~ ninety days to apply the Power of the Third Influence in your life.

Here's My Guarantee To You

If it doesn't turn your life around and make you more successful, I don't think you should have to pay for it. Just drop it in the mail and I'll refund your money.

But if you're like the others who've listened to this program, people will need a crowbar to pry your fingers off this set.

Warning! Lend this set to your friends at your own risk; you may never see it returned!

Quick, Easy, and Inexpensive

The *Secrets of Creating Wealth* contains my ultra-secret formulas for developing an **instant success mindset**.

But this sweet deal won't last for long. I urge you to think of your dreams of success.

If you're not at the top yet, the *Secrets of Creating Wealth* will get your there in a jiffy.

In less than two minutes from now, your copy can be on its way to you. This may just be what you've been missing your entire life.

A Portion Of Your Order Will Be Donated To The Red Cross

When you order the *Secrets of Creating Wealth* audio, a portion of your order will be donated to the American Red Cross to aid in their Hurricane Katrina Relief Efforts. When you give the gift of Wealth to yourself, you will be giving the gift of life and first aid to those in need.

So take advantage of this special offer by going to:

www. Morgan-James.com/wealthaudio

And I'll see You At The Top!

Sincerely,

Stephen A. Pierce

Stephen Pierce

PS.   Remember, you have access to the same winner's mindset only available to my exclusive coaching members for less than 1% of what they had to pay. **Just $97** (plus shipping and handling) and it's on the way to you.

PPS.   I am NOT kidding about the guarantee. Take ninety days to put this program to the test. If you're not thrilled with your purchase, just let me know for a quick, hassle free refund.

PPPS.   We've been contacted by a huge online company that listened to a preview set of these CD's. They want our entire stock of CD's for their members. So you better grab your set before it's too late. Take advantage of this special offer RIGHT NOW at:

www. Morgan-James.com/wealthaudio

Contact Stephen Pierce at:

Stephen Pierce

2232 S. Main St. #421

Ann Arbor, MI 48103

Phone: (734) 741-8392

Fax: (734) 622-9733

Email: Secrets@PierceSupport.com